BIGFOOT STILL LIVES...

IN IDAHO

BY BECKY COOK

To my family – Thank you for loving
me in spite of my imperfections.
Thank you also for always encouraging
me to write down my stories and tell
them frequently.

Good timber does not grow with ease
The stronger the wind,
The stronger the trees.

CONTENTS

WITH THANKS TO:
KIM - FOR AMAZING COUNSEL AND
FOR KEEPING MY HEAD ON
STRAIGHT.
GYDA -FOR BEING A LISTENING EAR
FOR ALL OF MY IDEAS.
MIKE- FOR BELIEVING IN ME

AND A SPECIAL **THANKS** TO
BRANDON TENNANT FOR DOING
AN AMAZING JOB ON THE COVER
FOR THIS BOOK.

BIGFOOT STILL LIVES...

IN IDAHO

FORWARD

My purpose in writing this book isn't to prove or disprove the existence of Bigfoot, but rather to offer graphic evidence in the form of eyewitness stories that they exist for those who choose to believe.

Many folks I talk to have said that the whole Bigfoot phenomenon is a hoax, that there can't possibly be a Bigfoot as there isn't any tangible evidence. I know otherwise; that there have been visual sightings by reputable, honest, sober folks and there is corroborating evidence - footprints, vocal samples, and hair samples.

For those who have had their own sightings - you don't need more proof, you already know. It is incredibly amazing to have validation of an otherwise unusual experience though, and that is what this book offers.

For those who want to know more - there are websites devoted to the compilation of data - footprints, pictures, sounds and hair samples. This book just offers additional information.

For those of you who choose not to believe - what are you doing reading this book?
If we all are crazy then you just joined the ranks.
Welcome to the land of Bigfoot Believers!

In my first book, Bigfoot Lives in Idaho, I told the story that started my collection of Bigfoot stories. Since that time I have had other experiences as I have further explored the Bigfoot world. It is fascinating to me and to others, to see inside a world that is similar to ours yet different in many aspects.

Palisades

When my family goes camping we play in the river most of the day, eat a lot of meals cooked over a fire in a Dutch oven, and later in the day we read out loud.

On one particular camping trip I was reading our current favorite book until almost midnight when my voice started to crack and I realized it was time to quit for the night and go to sleep. I encouraged the family to go to bed and made sure everything was taken care of for the night and then crawled into my own tent. I was just settling down well when I heard something outside the tent near the picnic table. I realized then that I had neglected to take care of the vegetable peelings from our last Dutch oven meal and was seriously kicking myself, thinking that my actions had most likely attracted some unwanted attention from the animal population.

I carefully unzipped the tent zipper and peered outside to the area near the picnic table where I saw what I first supposed must be a skunk or badger. It had a darker body with a lighter colored stripe down its back and it was bent over the scraps so my mind drew the conclusion – badger or skunk. That would have been a safe conclusion except for the fact that the back of it was even with the top of the picnic table, and it was

3

indeed bent over just as we would bend over to pick something up off the ground.

Looking back, I am not sure what got into me but I yelled, "What are you doing in our camp?" and immediately the Bigfoot (and I am positive this is what it was) took off. He put one fist down on the ground like a linebacker and just started running from that position, making three full strides before he was lost in the woods around camp.

When situations like this happen and we see or experience things that don't quite match up with any other experience we have yet categorized in our brain, we tend to stash it away inside somewhere - it just doesn't make sense, so we either don't think about it or we disregard it. In these days of computer technology we might google it until we come to some sort of conclusion. Back then we didn't have that type of technology and I discredited what I saw in my own mind, thinking I must have been excessively tired. Surely what I saw was some type of an animal, I just didn't know what. Eventually I forgot about what I saw until I was starkly reminded one day.

Years later when I started on this journey with the Bigfoot I realized that what I saw was a juvenile Bigfoot who probably was listening to the story I read as it was most interesting. In my experience with them I have found them to be very curious about us as humans and often when we are out in the woods, they are too.
One thing that I tell people when I teach is that we need to return to the time of mutual respect for all things in nature (including people) that once existed in this world, years ago. Respect is critical as it allows the

Bigfoot the space to contact us when needed. It is also important for our own good as humans especially as we as a people become more modernized and more advanced so that we realize that there are other worlds out there and some of them bump very closely against ours.

The Bigfoot are bigger and stronger than we are and yes, they are capable of doing many amazing things. But I have found in collecting these stories that if we allow them the opportunity to be friendly and approach us in their own fashion, they will.

Always remember that Bigfoot are not human beings, they are their own type of beings and they can't be credited with human reactions. I have found that they will respond similar to us in some situations, but most often not as they are their own people with their own way of life.

Dale Graham is a big guy who ran into a bigger guy – Bigfoot. He saw him up close and personal and there was no mistaking what he saw or what he looked like. The smell was amazingly rank and when he returned to the area later he found a lot of footprints, some of which are included in this book.

Basin Patch

Dale Graham is a big guy, but after running into a Bigfoot who was bigger, he is a little leery of the outdoors.
It was 1999 and Graham was out chopping wood south of Oakley, Idaho towards Basin Patch. He had just finished cutting down a bunch of trees and was loading them into his truck when he started smelling something rank.

"I thought at first I was smelling something that had winter killed," he said. "Then I got to wondering why I hadn't smelled it before when I was cutting the trees down."

He straightened up and turned to look around and came face to face with a large, male Bigfoot about ten feet away. He said it was tall – between seven and eight feet tall as Graham, who is six two, was looking straight into his very broad, hairy chest. Its hair was very dark, almost black, and must have weighed about 4-500 pounds.

"He scared me bad – he could have popped me like a blackhead," Graham said. "He had a massive chest. He dwarfed me."

He said he averted his head, not wanting to make eye contact with the Bigfoot, and when he next glanced up the creature was walking away like a tired old man.

"In my mind, I can still see how he looked, walking away from me," Graham said. "He stretched out his arm and pushed aside a tree and went up the hill."

The experience shook him so much that he left pretty abruptly, leaving some of his gear behind on the hillside. Three weeks later he went back with some other folks to see if they could find tracks. They found Graham's grease gun right where he left it, but they also found over a hundred footprints all over the hillside, most of which were 16 and 17 inches long, but also some smaller ones as well. (See picture in rear of book)

Seeing Bigfoot has definitely changed his life since then.

"I used to love going up to the mountains to get wood. If I heard of a neighbor needing wood, I was on it," he said. "But now, you know, I don't want to go up as often – even when someone else is with me."

He said that as he has thought about that experience, he thinks that the loading of the truck – with the wood knocking together over and over - might have been taken as tree knocking and could have been the reason the Bigfoot was attracted to him.

"He was really smelly," Graham said. "You know how the male elk will spray themselves during mating season? I kind of think that was why he smelled."

He said his initial thought was that the whole experience was scary.

Graham said that folks have tried to tell him he must have imagined what he saw or misidentified what he saw. He disagrees.

"There is no misidentification. I was too close."

He said that his whole perspective of life has changed, and seeing Bigfoot has shifted the way he thinks about life.

"Seeing Bigfoot will do that to you…"

This particular story happened a long time ago, but it's still a fun story. This particular episode became part of the Schut family history and was retold many times after it happened.

Challis

The fall colors were turning bright as Lucille and Herman Schut brought their horses down from the mountains. They made this trip periodically, bringing horses down from Loon Creek off the Yankee Fork. The Schuts hadn't been married long; it was his first marriage, her second. At forty, he was eleven years her senior, just back from the war, a crusty old mountain man at heart. He had lived up in the mountains alone for a long time, had seen and done a lot of things. He wasn't afraid of anything.

When they brought the horses down strange things always happened. While Herman was used to them, Lucille was not.

"We had one horse that just couldn't stay with the rest of the herd," she told her son, Paul. "Every day it would run off and keep its distance."

Then one day after settling in by the fire for the night they heard a horse scream and moments later the horse came running in. It arrived near the fire by the humans and stood there, shaking. No amount of pressure from the Schuts could induce it to move away from the humans for the rest of their trip. Just then, from out of the nearby hills, an eerie wail came forth.

"It was high and long, like nothing I have ever heard before," Lucille Schut said.

11

Her husband felt that it must be some type of cougar in distress or maybe an elk with a bad cold. He figured it must have gotten close enough to the horse to spook it good. Whatever it was, it just didn't sound right.

Fast forward nearly fifteen years. The Schuts are sitting in a crowded theatre watching a commentary with a reenactment of Sasquatch.

"The whole thing was pretty fake. I mean, you could tell these guys were in costume," she said. "Then near the middle they played a recording from the one Sasquatch they claimed to have trailed."

That one scream made the hair stand up on the back of her neck and immediately brought to her mind the night with the horses, years past.

"It was the exact same scream," she said. "There was no mistaking that noise anywhere."

It's one of those memories that stick in your brain for years, as evidenced by the many people who have had similar experiences. You might not be able to categorize what you heard when you initially hear it, but you never forget it. Eventually, someday, the answer appears and for many, finding out that what they heard or saw was a Bigfoot actually brings closure to an unsettling experience.

John Melland enjoys camping and in the last few years has had a few adventures with the local Bigfoot in the general Boise area. Some of these experiences have happened when he was with his family and sometimes they happened when he was alone, or so he thought…

He first saw Bigfoot in Oregon back in 1976 when he was pretty young, but the impression stayed with him. Over the years his family had talked about their own Bigfoot experiences and he always keeps his eyes open for more time with the big guy when he is out in the woods.

Crouch

The first time John Melland saw a Bigfoot in Idaho he was at the Boiling Springs campground north of Crouch, ironically on Halloween night, 2009. He and his wife had been sitting around the campfire talking and enjoying the warmth of the campfire. About eleven he noticed a tall dark figure standing at the trailhead between their fire and the main parking area for the campground. It first appeared between two trees, sometimes standing still, sometimes swaying back and forth. There was a nearly full moon that night and it stood there for a long time- maybe fifteen or twenty minutes. He and his wife were the only ones at the campground and it seemed strange for someone human to be standing there for such a long period of time, but it didn't look human, more like a large gorilla. It definitely wasn't a bear…

There wasn't a breeze and there wasn't any smell, and neither Melland nor his wife heard anything in spite of the fact that it was standing on gravel. Eventually, it just faded away.

13

The next year it happened again in the same camping spot at about the same time of the year. This time there was a little snow on the ground and it was a little after midnight when they both started having the feeling that they were being watched. Then Melland got a feeling that something was wrong.

"It was a bad feeling," he said. "So I told my wife a fib and said I was really cold and wanted to go home. I didn't want to alarm her."

As they were loading things up into the car they heard a loud boulder hit the ground about 50 yards away with a loud and distinct sound. That really shook them both and they loaded their car even faster. After they were loaded, they drove around a bit, but couldn't see anyone or anything but they decided to go on home that night.

The next camping trip took the Melland family up to Willow Creek campground in August 2010 for a camping, swimming, and fishing trip. They were really enjoying the cool breezes after the heat of the valley and had a great first day. In the middle of the night about 2:30, Melland's wife woke him up and told him to listen.

Outside the tent they could hear wood knocking coming from three different locations, one across the river from where they camped. The knocks didn't seem to be in any set pattern and they would hear two, three, or four knocks before the next one a little further away would respond.

"It was a distinct wood on wood knock and quite loud," he said. "We both knew the Bigfoot was out there."

The area they were in is steep with rocky outcropping on the mountain surrounding the campground. It would be very improbable for people to be walking around the steep mountainside at that time in the morning.

Two years later Melland was back at this same campground and heading to the restroom late at night when a throw rock hit a tree about ten feet from him about the level of his head.

"It sounded like a good sized rock," he said. "I turned on my headlamp and looked around, but didn't see anything. I thought it might be one of my stepsons messing with me, but they were at our camp. I went scouting around the next day to look for tracks, but the ground was too dry and hard to yield anything."

He said that he has found tracks several times, but so far hasn't found any that would lend themselves to being cast clearly. One set was near Boiling Springs campground, about fifteen inches long and the stride was about twice what his was going downhill.

"Once I find a good set of prints I plan on casting them," he said.

Sometimes when you are driving you catch sight of something out of the corner of your eye and will wonder is you really saw what you thought you saw. In this case, Gary Metz was a passenger as his father in law was driving and he was sure he saw what he saw.

Chesterfield

In November 2002 Gary Metz and his father in law were headed towards Chesterfield and had just turned off US 30 after coming over from Lava Hot Springs. They made the turn off and were traveling along when Metz saw a Bigfoot go right up the hill beside them.

"He was real quick," Metz said. "He was really big and tall. He was brown with long hair and looked to be over seven feet tall."

Metz is a big guy also – standing at six feet two, but this Bigfoot appeared bigger and could likely have been much larger than he originally thought. He said that his overall impression was that it looked like an ape only running upright – definitely not bear-like. His father in law wasn't inclined to stop and have a look around and at the rate the Bigfoot was traveling, it would have been well over the hill by the time they stopped.

"It was only about 300 yards away, but it was traveling so quickly I only saw it for a brief moment of time," Metz said. "It wasn't a bear, it was standing too tall."

The area there is made up almost entirely of sage brush and he said he saw it in the morning.

"If there is a Bigfoot, he probably lives there by Inman or Chesterfield," Metz said. "As fast as it was traveling it could be anywhere as it was traveling – covering four feet at a time."

He said that a few years later they were up in the Wolverine area snowmobiling in deep, deep snow and he found tracks out in the middle of nowhere.

"If I had stepped off my sled the snow would have been up to my armpits," he said. "You couldn't see distinct footprints, but I remember thinking that no human would logically be out here in the snow in the middle of nowhere…"

There is an area on I-15 between the small town of Inkom and the bigger town of Pocatello where the road narrows and goes between two pieces of a lava flow. It's called Black Rock and there have been multiple Bigfoot sightings near there over the last few decades. Above Black Rock sits a formation known by locals as Chinese Peak where there is an old gold mine. It was here that Mike William's relationship with the Bigfoot begins and has continued with several experiences that just keep him looking for the big guy.

Chinese Peak

Mike Williams was just twelve years old the day he saw his first Bigfoot. His family lived near Black Rock, south of Pocatello and he was near the back door of the house when a movement caught his eye. It came from a small canyon to the side of their home, an area that had dogwoods, deer and a small spring, yet with really steep sides. Out of this canyon came a very tall, very black Bigfoot, moving right along.

"I grabbed my dad's binoculars and sat on the back steps and watched him as he came down the canyon," Williams said. "His arms seemed much longer than they should be."

He said it turned and went up an old forest service road up the mountain, and he watched it until it disappeared from sight.
He said that he immediately went in and told his dad, but he didn't believe him.

"He told me not to start that crap…"

19

He said that later his father tried to convince him it was a really tall hiker. Williams might have believed that at one point in his life but not now.

"He might have been a really tall hiker who went up into the mountains," he said. "But he was in an area where it is difficult to climb and he went past an old cedar tree on the way up. I have hiked up to that old cedar tree and it is easily 4 feet tall – the Bigfoot just towered over it!"

Williams was a typical boy who liked to explore all over the mountain with friends. About this time there were people camped out at the top of Chinese Peak, mining in the old gold mine.

"My mom told us not to go up there," Williams said. "They were just old drunk hippies."

Being a curious kid, he kept an eye on them and then one day they were just gone.

"We kids went up there to poke around and they had just left everything there – sleeping bags, food, and a nice rock pick," he said. "It looked like something had scared them and they just run off and left everything, we made quite the haul once we realized they weren't coming back."

Shoup

A couple of years later when Williams was a teenager of about seventeen he went hunting with his family. They were camped up near Shoup on Spring Creek.

"We were supposed to be deer hunting, but my brother was being a stinker so we came back to camp," he said.

It was almost lunch time, so they decided to stop hunting to fix something to eat. Williams went into the camper to make sandwiches and his cousin, a big football player, went to get their pop out of the cooler for lunch. The cooler was about fifty feet from the creek and the cousin was just bending over to reach inside when he saw something in the creek.

"He ran back to the camper, came inside and slammed and locked the door. He was just shaking and almost in tears he was so upset. He said there was a wild animal out there," Williams said. "I questioned him – what was it? A deer, an elk, a bear?"

He told Williams that he had been at the cooler getting the pop, and he slammed the lid. Immediately there was motion in the water near him and he glanced up to see a being, kneeling down in spring creek, drinking. His sudden motion at the cooler startled it so that it stood up suddenly and just walked up the mountain.

"My cousin was a big 17-year-old who was really confident – he acted like he carried the whole world on his shoulders," Williams said. "It scared him to death, but he probably scared it too. Later on in his life he tried to convince me that he had only seen a deer, but what deer makes a big guy like that sweat so hard and nearly cry?"

Spring Creek
The next time he encountered something was in 1976 and the family was once again up Spring Creek. They

had stopped near Frenchman's Flat and everyone had a sandwich and a pop, just resting.

"We were in an area where there is black timber so thick they look like hairs on a dog's back," he said. "We could smell a sudden stench like nothing I have ever smelled before or since – absolutely rank. It was very overpowering."

His father said, "We need to get out of here," so they left the area, not knowing what was out there, just knowing it made everyone in the party uneasy.

He said he has been up in the same area several times since then, once when he heard a blood curdling scream coming up the canyon. He couldn't see what caused that then either, but would recognize it as being unusual, and at that time he thought it was from a Bigfoot.

"I didn't see him that time either," he said." I keep looking and maybe one of these days I will see him again."

He said that he has changed the way he does things since have those experiences.

"I don't hunt anymore," he said. "I prefer to take a video camera and stay near the camper when my family goes up in the mountains. I have found that I would rather take pictures than kill something."

He also can't deny what he has seen.

"Bigfoot could easily live up in Salmon area," he said. "There are places up there that no man has ever touched."

22

Looking for Bigfoot is like looking for a needle in a haystack – but it's a very big haystack and the needle is moving

Kim Marston enjoys hearing stories about Bigfoot, but he has also had his own experience.

City of Rocks

It's been a while since Kim Marston had contact with a Bigfoot, and at the time he wasn't sure what it was, he just knew it wasn't cattle.

"My wife and I were camping out up in the City of Rocks about 35 years ago when we both had a feeling we were being watched," Marston said. "The hair was standing up on the backs of our necks."

He said that they had planned to sleep outside under the stars that night but decided against it when they both continued to feel unsettled. Instead they slept in a tent they had rigged in the back of their pickup.

"During the night we heard someone walking around outside, great big - Thump, Thumps," he said. "We thought it might have been cattle as there were cattle out there, but they don't make the distinctive sound that people walking on two feet do and that is what we heard."

He said there was a pasture behind their pickup, but between the pasture and the truck there was a big rock and they heard the Bigfoot as he walked around the rock formation. The next day when they went out to investigate the area they found the weeds were knocked down in the pattern of big footprints.
"I honestly can't say I have seen Bigfoot," Marston said. "But there was something out there and it wasn't cattle."

25

It was early spring when Lorena Seaton's cousin invited her to take a ride in their grandpa's beat up old pickup truck. Her fourteen year old cousin had just barely received her driving license that day and wanted to take the truck for a spin – they could go anywhere they wanted just as long as she got to drive. They decided to head east out of town to their grandpa's old sheep camp as they knew he had just stocked it up and they were looking for some cookies. It seemed like a good idea at the time.

Driggs

It was the middle of a spring day, and Lorena Seaton was just twelve, when her fourteen year old cousin got her driver's license and offered to take them both for a drive in their grandpa's old beat up pickup.

"My grandpa had this old sheep camp that he used to keep really well stocked in case he had to use it," she said. "We were just going over to get some cookies out of it."

Looking back, she said she was sure that her grandpa knew all of the grandkids knew where he kept his cookies, but he just kept stocking them.
The sheep camp was parked inside a field east of Driggs near a place they called Three Creeks. To get there the kids had to stop and open a gate, then pull straight in alongside a long hay stack. The only way back out of the field was to turn around in a big circular area and go back through the same gate that they came in. The sheep camp was normally parked in the center of the circular area.

On the road to the field, there was a turn off towards a community dump and the kids had been warned not to go over that way alone as there were sometimes hobos or vagrants.

"We had just always been warned not to go over there as our parents just didn't know how the people would act," Seaton said.

They arrived at the gate to the field and Seaton got out to open it, and as she opened the door she smelled a horrible odor. She initially thought it was a sheep that had died.

"I said 'oh no, grandpa has another dead sheep', then I opened the gate and just hopped back into the pickup," Seaton said.

They drove into the field and as they approached the sheep camp, they could see that everything from inside the camp had been thrown out on the ground around it. Immediately they thought it must have been the result of one of the hobos and Seaton's cousin asked her what they should do.

"Gun it," came the reply. "I didn't even know what that really meant," she said. "I was just a twelve-year-old who had heard other people say that."

She said her cousin put her foot down on the gas and they just belted around the sheep camp and took the turn that would return them back down the road home. Just as they rounded the sheep camp, they both saw a tall, white Bigfoot standing pressed against the end of the hay stack.

"He was almost as tall as the hay stack – about eight or nine feet tall. He had long hair all over his body, but not as much on his face or across his chest as you could see his chest through his hair," she said. "He didn't seem to be old, but his hair was white with a yellow shine to it. He had dark hands, and it was definitely a male judging from the way his chest looked."

He had long arms, longer than what a man would have, she said, and appeared startled and scared at the same time.

"He didn't have an ape like head – it was taller and more square than an ape's head," she said. "More like what Chewbacca looks like in Star Wars than the Bigfoot in the Patterson Gimlin film."

It was one of those moments when the memory exists as though captured in a frozen moment in time.

"We were moving past him and back down the road when I turned to my cousin and said, 'Did you see that?' We both looked back, but by then he must have run behind the haystack because we couldn't see him anymore."

She said that they really had that pickup moving by then and they didn't even stop to shut the gate as they raced toward her home. They were going so fast they only narrowly averted an accident on the way home and when they got there they ran in to tell their parents what they had seen. Unfortunately, their parents didn't believe them.

"We were both pretty upset," she said. "But the parents all laughed and said what big imaginations we had."

Years later when she was in her late teens and early twenties she would go out in the same area to snowshoe in the middle of the night and often felt that there was someone watching her, but she didn't ever feel threatened. When she spoke with one of her old neighbors, they validated her experience and let her know that a member of their family had also seen the same white Bigfoot five different times in the same area.

"This old grandpa has since passed on but it helped me feel better about what we saw," she said.

It's an experience that she hasn't shared with many people.

"I have never seen a Bigfoot before that or since then, but even now I think of it as one of the special things that happen just once in my life," she said. "I always felt there was something out there, but it wouldn't hurt me."

Wesley Southwood is another young man who had a very cool experience with Bigfoot, but this experience just happened two years ago.

Fish Haven

Wesley Southwood, his father, and his brother go hunting for elk every year in the same place – the high valley areas above Bear Lake in the vicinity of Fish Haven. In 2013 they were up in that area, walking across a snowfield, when he had his first Bigfoot sighting.

"We were walking across this field, with my dad and brother ahead of me a little bit," he said. "I heard something behind me and turned around and saw this big brownish-white Bigfoot stand up and walk away."

He said that when they first walked through that area, he thought what he was seeing was a big rock with either moss or snow on it. But rocks don't walk away…

"It was squatting down in the snow," he said. "It might have been eating something. But it took off and walked away into the tree line about a hundred feet away. It took really long strides."

He said that he was scared because it was huge, but even now he isn't sure just how tall it was - possibly as big as eight or ten feet tall. He said that he watched it as it walked up on a bank of sage brush and then went into a tree line to the point where it just blended in with the trees and disappeared.

31

For something so big, Bigfoot can cover a lot of ground fast. Speed was the overall impression when one woman living on the reservation had an experience with a Bigfoot.

Fort Hall

Danny Elderidge grew up on the Shoshone Bannock Indian Reservation where they moved around a lot. About the time she was in the third grade her family moved to a home on Gay Mine road, near Mount Putnum.

"I was sitting outside on the front porch with the rest of the kids when I heard what sounded like a huge pack of dogs fighting," she said. "It sounded awful and then we heard a screaming yell like a dog was being ripped in half and it echoed off the side of the hill."

It was enough to make a huge impression on her and she never forgot what she heard. Years later she was once again living on the reservation when she had another odd experience.
It was late at night and her kids were all in bed when she happened to glance out the back window and there was something that looked like a big bush in her yard.

"At first I just thought that there was something wrong with what I was seeing and then I realized that there was something there that shouldn't have been there. It looked like a big bush, except I don't have a bush in my yard," she said. "Then it stood up. It was HUGE, black, and very fast."

She said that she immediately thought it would be a good idea to shut the window and the blind and was attempting to do that when the Bigfoot began to run around her trailer.

"It sounded like a huge Clydesdale, thundering around the trailer," she said. "It was pounding on all of the sides of the trailer and standing up it was almost taller than the trailer. I can't even begin to express how terrified I was."

She said that it moved so fast that she thought it must have some type of mystical power.
By then her kids were up and in the living room and she joined them and the family dog, a Pitbull.

"He was shaking," she said.

A short time later the Bigfoot left and she did too, packing up her kids with what they could grab quickly, she went somewhere she thought might be safer. And then she moved away from that house that week.

"I wasn't about to go back to that house," she said. "I figured the Bigfoot could have it if he wanted it."

If you see your first Bigfoot when you are a little kid, it might scare you, a lot. That is what happened to Tiffany Nesbitt when she was 12 and she and her brother ran into one coming down a mountain. She isn't much older now, but that incident is ingrained in her memory as though it were yesterday.

Freeman Lake

Growing up in Idaho, Tiffany Nesbitt spent a lot of time during the summer at her dad's home on Freeman Lake. It was a beautiful place to be and she and her brother spent a lot of time outside. One fall day they had gone swimming in the lake and were riding their bikes home when they both heard a lot of rustling sounds coming down the mountain at a high rate of speed. They watched for about a minute as a black form came crashing down the mountain, the sounds getting louder and louder and coming closer. Suddenly a Bigfoot came crashing out of the trees and brush and jumped down off a ledge, to land on the road right in front of them.

"I think we scared him as much as he scared us," Nesbitt said. "He was huge, hairy, and scary and I peed my pants."

She said he was about eight and a half feet tall with muscly arms. While he had medium length black hair over his body, his face was a tannish color entirely covered by hair with yellow eyes. She describes his nose as being a different texture than a human nose – more like a dog or bear's nose, and kind of wrinkly. He didn't seem to be particularly old either.

35

"He had really broad shoulders," she said. "I think it was a male, but even now I am not sure about that."

She said that they got out of there pretty quick and went on home where she got her butt beat for peeing her pants, but eventually her dad went back with them to where they saw the Bigfoot.

"My dad saw the footprints where he (the Bigfoot) landed in the road," she said. "My dad was a big guy, about six foot five, but the prints made his feet look small."

She describes the area as being made up of trees and brush with a lot of berries they call thimbleberries that are like raspberries.

"You can't see much when you look up that hill," she said. "There is too much thick brush, which is why we couldn't see the Bigfoot until he landed in front of us – he just looked like something black coming down the hill."

Nesbitt said that the area has the best wild strawberries on the planet, but she won't go pick strawberries alone or go out to the lake alone anymore.
She said prior to this experience she and her brother had built a two story fort in a tree on the mountain behind and above their house. They spent a lot of time out there, but about a week after they finished building it, they found it completely ripped apart – nails and everything. Nesbitt said that she thinks now that Bigfoot ripped the tree house apart.

"I don't know why it would rip it apart," she said. "But I will never forget it being destroyed."

She said that they still go out into the woods to hunt and she has heard the Bigfoot "Whoop" but says that they don't make the sound that she has heard on TV. She has also heard them make another sound similar to a "beep".

"One of the last times we were out there we heard the beep coming from three different sides," she said. "I am sure it is them – there isn't anything else out there that could possibly make that noise."

There have been numerous Bigfoot sightings around the Blackfoot and Gibson areas so it is no surprise to find even more. These all happened to one person, Rachel Gold and they are amazing.

Gibson

It was September 1996 and school had just started for the year the day that Rachel Gold decided to sneak some cigarettes out to the family tree house to smoke them.

"I was being naughty, I was still a teenager," she said. "I was up in the tree house smoking and looking out over the field when I saw someone walking in the field up towards the homes."

She said he came up between two houses and she wondered where he was going. And then she noticed that he didn't have any clothes on.

"He was only about twenty feet away and I could see it clearly against the yellow of the field," she said. "I was kind of scared, so once it passed, I got down and ran into the house and got my brother and sister as my parents weren't home."

She describes it as being a tall and lanky juvenile with dark brown hair lying flat against its head.

"I couldn't tell how tall it was from the angle I was at in the tree house, but I had seen several Bigfoot before this," she said. "They were older ones that were more massive and muscular."

She said that they had a fruit orchard and when she first saw the Bigfoot it appeared between two apple trees.

"There are lots of places for it to go," she said. "We had apples and gooseberries there so I think it came from the orchard area."

She was living in the same area a short time later when she had another experience, this time with her sister.

"We used to walk to the nearest store, but there were lots of thorns," Gold said. "So this time we took our bikes, but they picked up the thorns and had flat tires."

It was getting late, about 9 o'clock and about dusk and she was expected home so they left the bikes near the only light by the canal and started walking home, cutting across on the canal road.

"There is only one light and it was pretty dark," she said. "As we came up near where there is a waterfall into the canal we could hear a weird humming sound that we had never heard before."

She said as they got closer to the waterfall the sound was getting louder and louder but it didn't sound scary.

"Our eyes were getting used to the dark and we could clearly see the Bigfoot standing in the waterfall," she said. "It didn't see us and we didn't stop."

She said that the water came to its shoulders so she couldn't tell if it was male or female, but it had to be pretty strong to stand where it was standing.

"The water there is at least six feet deep where the canal company dredges out the canal and there is a pretty good undertow so only a strong swimmer can stay under the water where it comes off the hill," she said. "It was hot and we were in tank tops, shorts, and sandals. I am sure it was just enjoying getting wet and cooling off."

They ran home and told their parents what they saw and their parents told them to just leave it alone.

"We would actually see the Bigfoot a lot when I was younger," she said. "When we would camp outside in a tent we would hear them walk around. We were told to just leave them alone and they would leave us alone."

She said that they even had one come in their house once when she and her mom and step dad were planning on watching a movie.

"It was one of those hot days in the summer when we had all the doors open. We had popped some popcorn and my mom and I were sitting on the couch waiting to start the movie," she said. "I saw someone go thru into the kitchen."

She said she initially thought it was her step dad that they were waiting for but he was in the bedroom.

"On the way out it peeked in at us and then left," she said. "I think it came in because it smelled the popcorn. It was about man sized, but was younger – it just peeked and left."

When the canal would dry up each year a group of the neighborhood kids would go up and spear the fish left in the puddles in the canal. The last time they did that they had rocks thrown at them.

"My step dad said that the Bigfoot needed food too, and we should leave the fish," she said. "So we didn't go up after that."

One very memorable experience happened when she was yet again being naughty and playing hooky with some other kids. They were pretty careful not to get caught so they drove their pickup in the hills and went hiking for the day.

"We were hiking around when we found a cave that was obviously someone's home," she said.
It had some pretty cool improvements.

"On the front of the cave was this little porch with a woven roof over it made of trees and branches tied together with shrubs piled on top like a sun porch," she said. "It wasn't very big – only three of us could stand there comfortably."

Inside the cave there was a trench that had been dug out and filled with hay that looked comfortable. There were pretty stones placed in specific positions.

"Like someone was decorating with them, like ornaments," she said. "The floor was hard packed, and there wasn't a sign of a fire anywhere."

She said they were only in there a few minutes when she started feeling very uneasy, but not scared.

"I told my friends we needed to leave," she said. "This was very clearly someone else's home and we were violating it."

While Gold's experiences are pretty cool, they aren't really unusual in her family. Her grandmother, who passed away at the age of 94, had an ongoing relationship with the resident Bigfoot family near her.

"She would talk to them in Shoshone and they would scare away anyone who wasn't supposed to be there," Gold said.

She said that her grandmother lived in an older house that had a wood stove to cook on and heat with and still had an outhouse 40 feet behind the home. The family actually built her a newer home but she preferred to live in the old house so each year the family would get together to cut enough wood for her needs. One particular time they dropped the wood off in the center of the yard with plans to come back and stack it the following day. However, when they returned the next day all of the wood was already stacked neatly.

"She said that the Bigfoot stacked it for her," Gold said. "They would also clear a pathway from her doorway to the outhouse when it was snowy outside."

She said that her grandmother wanted to share more about the relationship she had with the Bigfoot, but at the time Gold was a busy teenager and didn't want to pay attention, something she really regrets now. She does remember some of the lessons her grandmother taught her though.

"They like music and they love to watch us," she said. "They will let you know if you should follow them. They were never mean though, our horses never freaked out around them."

Wade Johnson has lived down by the little town of Inkom since 1965. He is very familiar with the area around him and has hunted all over. His experience with Bigfoot happened back behind the Black Rock area on what is known as the old road from Inkom to Pocatello or Buckskin Road.

Inkom

Wade Johnson, his brother, and a good friend were out hunting in the fall of 1978. It was early afternoon and the hunters had split up to hunt over the mountain when Johnson came across his first Bigfoot.

"I came down over the ridge and saw this Bigfoot, standing in a Juniper tree, scratching his back," Johnson said. "He was shaking that tree like a twig."

He said that the tan Bigfoot was tall enough that his head was in the thinning top of the tree and he was really scratching hard as the tree was just moving all over.

"It didn't look like a bear," he said. "I would guess it was about eight feet tall or so."

He said he snuck down to where he could get a better look, but by the time he came up closer to it, it was gone. About then he started getting fairly nervous and ran back over the ridge to where his buddy was.

"I just wanted there to be two of us, in case I saw it again," he said. "No one else in our group saw anything but they saw the look on my face and knew that it made an impression on me."

The following year in the fall, he was driving in the same area when he saw another Bigfoot, this time crossing the road in front of him.

"It was about nine o'clock at night after dark and I saw him run across the road, bent over like a running back," he said. "I kept asking myself 'did I just see what I thought I saw?'"

He said it was so quick that it was across the road in a flash. All he really knew for sure was that it appeared to be dark brown or black.

"I stopped the car and looked," he said. "I was asking myself if I wanted to get out and look around, but I talked myself out of it."

He said that after all of these years, he is still hopeful he will see Bigfoot again.

"I am still looking. I always carry my camera with me now," he said. "I figure whatever lottery you enter, you will win sometime."

When you are young and see a Bigfoot, that impression stays with you a long time. Such is the case with Von Hickman, who was with a friend when they were both about 13 years old and watched a Bigfoot cut across a hill slightly above them.

Island Park

Von Hickman was in Island Park camping with a good friend, an experience that happened several times a summer when he was younger. It was late July or early August in 1977, about 10:30 or 11 in the morning and they were out exploring up a creek when they both saw something they were sure wasn't a bear.

"We were walking up one of the creeks when we both saw something that wasn't a bear," Hickman said. "Bears don't move upright on their hind feet for long periods of time."

He said that they were about 3-400 yards away when they saw the Bigfoot walk across the brush and ghost into the trees in the higher ground above them.

"We watched it walk across a clearing for about a hundred yards," he said. "He had a long, striding gait and was a darker chocolate brown. I think he was just passing through as he didn't look around or see us; he just focused on where he was walking."

He said that they didn't hear anything and were too far away to smell anything.

47

"It didn't really scare us, but it did freak us out a little bit," Hickman said. "We hurried back to camp after seeing it though."

He said that both he and his friend were of the opinion that life exists elsewhere, that we as humans are always making new discoveries, and this experience kind of solidified that belief. They didn't really talk a lot about this experience and he said that since that time in his life he has lost contact with that friend. That doesn't change his belief about what he saw then though.

"I've been out in the woods a lot in the last fifteen years and I haven't seen anything like that since then," he said. "I still believe that I saw a Bigfoot."

Some of the best Bigfoot stories come from people who love to spend time in the mountains. Shane Hayes is one of those people. He loves to trap and hunt and consequently spends a lot of time out in the woods. During several of those trips he has had some pretty cool experiences with Bigfoot.

LOCKSA

"Most of my experiences have been on the Montana border near Locksa," Shane Hayes said.

He said he was following mule deer and dropped into a draw and the trees started shaking around them. And then the screams started.

"It was a long, raspy scream," he said. "It was repeated over and over - very guttural with a lot of volume."

He said they didn't know what it was but they decided they didn't want to know what it was.

"In the same general area, we would hear a long drawn out yell like "Hey", drawn out 30-45 seconds," Hayes said. "The cattle around us would go quiet and still and my brother saw some flashes of light and we both heard laughing like a hyena."

He said it was eerie and it didn't feel right in that area.

"I don't go back there by myself anymore," he said.

He said that over the course of the many years up in the mountains, he has found several structures, but he hasn't really put a lot of thought into who built them or why they were built where they were.

"Bigfoot is kind of a guilty pleasure," he said. "I am not equipped to think about what they are; I just tend to avoid them."

He was up Stinking Creek near Palisades when he found some clear footprints in an area of about sixty feet of bare ground. Hayes is six foot five and over 300 pounds with size 13/14 boots and these prints were three to four inches longer than his boots and indented a half inch into the ground where Hayes left no indention himself.

On another trip on the Locksa river in north central Idaho floating in an area where the coast was made up of large boulders that had rolled down from up above.

"Opposite us several big boulders started rolling down the hill," he said. "For a good ten to fifteen minutes we could hear rocks rolling loud enough to be heard over the sounds of the river."

Hayes was fishing for salmon and his cousin who was with him was fooling around and made a whistle out of leaves and actually got it to whistle pretty well.

"After a bit he got a responding whistle from across the river," Hayes said.

The hillside was covered with the boulders and heavy chaparral, so they couldn't see what was responding to them, but he thought it was pretty cool all the same.

50

Wherever you find mountains, you are sure to find Bigfoot, especially if there is a beautiful range with trees, water, and ample food. Such is the case on the Idaho Montana border as you go over Lolo Pass. Chuck Rogers was making this journey late at night when he saw a Bigfoot and that area haunts him still.

Lolo Pass

"My dad lived in Darby, Montana, about 25 miles north of the Idaho/Montana border on Hwy. 93," Rogers said. "I live in Filer, Idaho, about a five and a half or six hour drive away. When I went to visit him, I could only stay the day because he lived in a small one bedroom cabin. I would get up there in the morning, stay the day and head back about 10:00 pm. I'd drive to Salmon and get a room at a motel, and then head back to Filer in the morning."

In January of 2009, he left his dad's place to head back to Filer. It had snowed a few days earlier so all of the roads had packed snow and there was about two or three feet of scraped snow along the sides of the road. From Darby, Montana to the top of the mountain at the border he did not pass or see any vehicles, the road was deserted on a calm winter night with no wind or clouds in the sky.

"The moon was so full, the stars so bright and the snow was so white that you could have shut off your headlights and drive by the moonlight, "he said. "As I started down the other side of the pass toward Salmon I came around about the third of fourth curve, and there was an area where a large amount of snow had

51

been knocked down into my lane, spreading out about 8 feet across the road."

Rogers had grown up in Minnesota and spent a lot of time playing in snowbanks and snowmobiling in Yellowstone, so he knew that a large animal had just broken onto the road. He figured if there had been any time lapse at all, another vehicle would have flattened the snow, but there weren't any fresh vehicle tracks – it was that fresh.
As he came to the next sharp left turn, he slowed down almost to a stop, thinking he would probably see elk standing in the road but instead as he glanced off to the left, he saw a Bigfoot walking up the hill.

"I saw an upright creature topping the 45 degree hill as it took the last couple of steps up the hill," Rogers said. "I stopped next to the footprints going up the hill and just sat there, stunned. I had just seen a Bigfoot!"

He said what amazed him was the size of its leg muscles. Even in the moonlight he could see the strength in its legs from 30-40 yards away.

"They were massive!" he said. "It was like looking at a horse's leg."

Even though it was covered in hair he could still clearly see the Bigfoot. He said its back shoulder blades stuck out a little, like a football player with shoulder pads, and it was a reddish brown in color. He was just amazed at the amount of muscling on the Bigfoot. There were no trees right there at all, nothing to hide behind, but Rogers said that even then, if there hadn't been a full moon he would have missed him completely.

"If the moon and snow had not been so bright I would not have been able to see the details let alone seen it at all," he said. "I turned my truck to face the hillside so I could get some pictures of the tracks as I carry my camera with me so I can take pictures of my dad and I."

He said he was now blocking both sides of the road where it narrows to a slender two lane, his headlights pointing up the hill where it disappeared and where the footprints clearly led uphill with the snowbank being about four feet high on both sides.

"The footprints were about eight inches wide and about fourteen to sixteen inches long about five feet apart," he said. "I could see about seven or eight footprints on the left of the road and about eight or nine on the right side of the road."

He said it looked like the same type of footprints you would find if an average person were to run across a football field, just running straight up a forty five degree hill.
That was the part that shook him the most.

"Seeing that this being could run up that hill in a matter of seconds I knew he could run down just as fast," Rogers said. "I wanted to get out of my truck, but I was too scared."

He said that he sat there with his 45 automatic pointed out the driver side window waiting for someone to drive past so he could show them what he saw and get some pictures. But after sitting there 10-15 minutes no one drove by and the fear started getting to him so he decided to keep heading down the mountain. He pulled into Salmon about 2:00 AM, setting his alarm for 5:00 AM., but he didn't get any sleep. He kept telling himself that he would just drive back up there to take some pictures of the tracks in the daylight, but then he realized that he had to be at work by ten and that left little enough time to get home.

"All the way back, I was so mad at myself for not having the courage to get out of the truck the night before," he said.

He said that the next time he drove up to Montana he made the decision to move his dad home to live with him in Filer so that he wouldn't have to drive that same stretch of road again in the dark.

"After hunting by myself for over 30 years I have sold my camper and no longer hunt anywhere near there," he said. "I've been to Vietnam and nothing really scares me, but that night I was sure scared."

Rowdy Davis is a former banker turned outfitter and guide, but initially he only did outfitting on the side. He has been all over the mountains in the backcountry near the Selway-Bitterroot Wilderness and Frank Church River of No Return Wilderness for many years. I found his story while tracking down other Idaho outfitters with similar experiences. He currently runs Big Timber Outfitters.

MOOSE CREEK

In Idaho if you want to travel in the backcountry, some of the best people to travel with are outfitters and guides. Rowdy Davis has been outfitting as a side business for a long time and back in the 1970's during the fall hunting season in September he was up in the Selway –Bitterroot Wilderness off of a ridge above Moose Creek. He and one of his employees were riding their horses single file down the trail early – the same trail they had come into camp on the night before. The trail was muddy and a little wet where a spring seeped out of the mountain.

"We were only about a mile from our camp," he said. "We were riding down the trail single file with me in front and him behind when we saw these footprints."

What they saw were some mighty big footprints– easily 14 or 15 inches long. They were clearly visible through the mud for twenty or thirty yards along the trail where the water ran across.

Initially, Davis thought that what they were seeing was grizzly tracks because they were so big, but at the time it was pretty rare to even hear of grizzly in the Selway area.

"I've seen a lot of bear tracks and these were huge for a bear," he said.

But in examining the prints they couldn't find any claw marks and it clearly looked like bare feet prints. He said that bears normally have a rounder footprint and that this was very clearly a bare footprint- but very large.

Davis said that he has heard of outfitters and guides who have had Bigfoot sightings and now he knows that he has joined their ranks.

Stewart Matthews is a neuro-muscular therapist - a very specialized muscle therapist, so when he saw Bigfoot, he used words familiar with his work to describe what he saw. The amazing thing was WHERE he saw him – near the busy I-15 freeway system.

Pocatello

Stewart Matthews is a neuromuscular therapist now, but in a prior life he was a Special Forces army member in Northern Ireland. Then when he came over to the United States, he worked as a carpet cleaner until he got finished through school. This particular day he had been to American Falls to clean a carpet and was on his way back home to Pocatello to drop off the carpet cleaning van and then pick up his own vehicle. He was excited as he was headed down to an event down in Utah and that was on the top of his mind. He drove onto the I-15 south bound ramp, heading to Utah, when he saw a Bigfoot walking near the freeway.

"It was black and huge, pushing seven feet easily," Matthews said. "He was walking using his quadriceps, and when he turned to look across the freeway, he turned his head and shoulders, not his neck like we would do."

He said that he has doubts even now that what he saw wasn't someone playing an elaborate hoax, after all, no one else has come forward with other stories of sightings so close into town.

"If you put a tall basketball player in a suit and teach them to walk like the video on the Bigfoot you might be able to create what I saw," he said.

He said that one thing that he has always questioned about the Bigfoot were how they, or anyone else for that matter, could hide in plain sight. He said that when he was in the army, he was taught that it was possible to stand under a streetlight in such a way that you can't be seen.

"I didn't believe that," he said. "I flat out didn't believe it, until a day shortly after Christmas one year when I was proven wrong and I was right on top of someone before I saw them."

He said his opinion has changed since that experience and now he believes otherwise.

"If those beings are experts in the wild," he said. "They probably know all of the tricks of using shade to their advantage. That makes a lot more sense."

Bigfoot – Hide and Go Seek Reigning champion

Back in 1986 Del Reed Bergeson and his wife Shareen went fishing up near the head of the Blackfoot River by Poison Creek when their sleep was interrupted one night by a noisy intruder. They didn't get much sleep after that and unfortunately, their trailer will never be the same.

Poison Creek

Del Reed Bergeson wanted to get some fishing in one fall so he took his 27 foot trailer, his wife and his two small dogs and off they went. They had the trailer pulled over away from all the other fishermen by the head of Blackfoot River near Poison Creek when late one night they were awakened by something rocking their trailer.

"It was the middle of the night about one or two when the trailer started rocking," Bergeson said. "It woke me up out of a sound sleep – it felt like a big cow was rubbing against it. I thought I would go out and see what was happening, but my wife said no, something really stunk, and she didn't think that was a good idea at all."

Their two black labs climbed under the bed with their tails between their legs, but Bergeson finally decided to just lie down and wait it out. Then the trailer started rocking harder, so he got up to see what he could see.

"I got up and got my pistol and by then the trailer was rocking good and hard," he said. "I was going to open the door, but just as I got to the door, something grabbed the door handle and pulled on it. Thank Heavens it was locked…"

He said at first he thought it was cattle rubbing on the trailer, but when the trailer was rocking so hard he knew it wasn't cattle. Eventually it quit and he lay back down.

"The next morning when I went to open the door, the door fell off its hinges," he said. "All of the screws on the frame where you close the door were stripped clear out."

Bergeson said at the time he didn't know what to think of their experience.

"I got up the next morning and looked around outside," he said. "There was no sign of cattle in the area and the ground was so hard there were no tracks to be found either. I looked around and asked the other campers if they heard or saw anything but no one had."

He said that the reaction of his two labs was strange also. He said if it had been a person or even a cow, the dogs would have said something, but they didn't make any sound, they just climbed under the bed.
Even now, years later, he is glad he didn't open the door.

"Everyone I spoke to near Blackfoot River said that it sounded like Bigfoot," he said. "I hadn't even thought of that at the time."

Idaho is a beautiful state with areas that are absolutely gorgeous. Red Fish Lake, near Stanley, is one such area. Travis Terry loves to hike in that area with his friends and family and has had three experiences with Bigfoot in the same area – and he has the amazing pictures to prove it!

Red Fish Lake

Travis Terry is an avid Bigfoot hunter; he loves to go looking and listening in the woods. He made three trips into the same area near Red Fish Lake in 2012, once in August and twice in September, and had some amazing experiences each time.

The first trip in the hills, he was hiking with his wife, Becky, his little brother Brad, older brother Steve, as well as his son and daughter. He was trying a little tree, knocking to see if he could get a response from a Bigfoot but didn't hear or see anything.

On the way out of the woods, there was a large tree ripped out and left along the trail.

"You could see that the tree had grown out of the side of a hill. The roots were twisted out, not cut, and it had previously grown at an angle," Terry said. "It was just lying in the trail, and it definitely wasn't there when we went up the mountain.

The next day they hiked up to Lake Cramer knowing it was their last day there. As he hiked with his wife, he noticed a beautiful area of the trail and thought to himself that if he were a Bigfoot, that is exactly where he would go. So he left the trail and climbed down the hill.

"Looking back on this now, I think it was an incredibly stupid thing to do," Terry said. "If I had been hurt it would have been difficult, if not impossible, to get me out of there."

He said while hiking down a ways, he heard an enormous crash that sounded as though it had been made on purpose. There was no residual echo or any indication about what made the noise or where it had come from.

He knew he needed to get going and get off the mountain so he set his camera on his shoulder and filmed the area around them as they walked out. It wasn't until later, when he had a friend take the film apart frame by frame, that he was able to see the amazing pictures he had taken, some of them showing what clearly looked like several Bigfoot. As he looked over the frames one by one, he could clearly see Bigfoot, moving slowly to remain out of his sight.

He was hooked. He convinced his wife to hike up there with him one more time to see if he could find tracks or anything. They were about three-quarters of the way up the mountain when they heard a boulder crashing down the mountain, or at least something that sounded like a boulder coming down the mountain.

"My wife was pretty spooked," Terry said. "I'm praying to see one (A Bigfoot), and she is praying we won't see one."

Eventually his wife convinced him that they needed to get down the mountain and he reluctantly agreed. He wanted to get one last look at the area off the trail that he previously hiked to so he left his pack with his wife and hiked down the hill. He found a bear track and decided to take a picture of that, but didn't realize until he tried to take it that his camera was set on video.

"I started to just take the picture, but then noticed the camera was set on video so I just lifted the camera up and slowly panned it around for about nine seconds," he said. "It was then that I got an amazing picture of a family of Bigfoot."

The last time Terry was able to get up in the mountains before the snow came down, he could only convince his brother-in-law to go with him. The trip was fairly uneventful, but they did find some large rocks that had been hefted out of the ground.

"They were big enough, there was no way a man could have lifted them," he said.

Further along the trail coming down, he found another full grown tree that had been taken out of the ground completely – roots and all – and leaned across the same trail they had just traveled up not more than twenty minutes prior when the tree was not on the trail.

"That was pretty amazing," Terry said. "The tree still had moist dirt on the roots. We took pictures of it."

Terry still loves to go hiking and Red Fish Lake is still a favorite destination, but it is getting a little harder to find people who will go up with him. They are more than a little concerned that if they run into Bigfoot Terry will want to meet him personally.

Bigfoot doesn't believe in YOU either

www.bigfootlives.info

The area outside Riggins is beautiful, a part of the Payette National Forest that is considered high desert. Some of the area is quite arid, but other parts have beautiful tree covered slopes and rocky areas where the Bigfoot can be found. Eddy Gipson was living in an area with a lot of natural beauty around him – a pond, fruit trees, walnut trees, and a grape arbor. He would often see deer out in the back yard, eating on his fruit trees and stealing grapes off the vine. He really enjoyed the idyllic mountain area around him. That is, until the peace started not being so peaceful. Apparently the local Bigfoot family wanted to make his acquaintance and they were pretty forceful about welcoming him to the neighborhood. Once he realized that they were friendly, he was able to have some cool interaction with them.

RIGGINS

How do you meet the local Bigfoot when you are too far out of town to have a Welcome Wagon? Move in and you will find out, at least, that is what happened to Eddy Gipson.

"I was staying in my fifth wheel outside of Riggins with a mountain in front of me and the Salmon river behind me," Gipson said. "It was pretty peaceful. I really enjoyed living there. But every couple of nights the trailer would move and weird things would happen. My jeep got moved around in the mud and occasionally when I pulled up to the trailer at night, the hair would stand up on the back of my neck."

Initially, he was pretty fearful, not knowing what he was dealing with. It's tough to be calm when you don't know what you are up against.

"I had a big spotlight out in the yard that stayed on all night long," Gipson said. "Each night before I went to bed I would shut the curtains so that I could actually sleep."

One particular night he was a little concerned that he couldn't see the light outside the windows on the tip out of his trailer. It's a big trailer – 40 feet long and over 18,000 pounds. There are three windows in the tip out with the top of the windows being a little over nine feet tall. He peered a little closer out the window and found himself looking directly into the big brown eyes of a Bigfoot who was bent over the window, his arm above him balanced on the top of the trailer. He was big and black and had a cone shaped head similar to a gorilla.

"I was freaked out," Gipson said. "I didn't know what the heck to do."

So he ran back into the back bedroom of his trailer and called a friend near Boise whom he thought might have an answer.

"He told me it was probably a Bigfoot, come to visit me," Gipson said. "He asked me if I had some peanut butter and I did. Then he told me to put it out on the front step and I told him he was crazy if he thought I was going out there while that big thing was there."

It took some convincing, but he finally, cautiously, opened the door while keeping his friend on the other

70

end of the phone, and set out a jar of peanut butter. As he quickly glanced around, he could see not one, but TWO Bigfoot, standing on his side of the river, but he had the impression that there was a third one standing near the two just out of sight.

Gipson's dog was inside the trailer in a kennel and seemed unconcerned by the whole visitation, however the neighbor's dog was going crazy with its barking and howling – and then it abruptly stopped and there was complete silence.

"I stayed on the phone with my friend most of the night," he said. "The next morning I went out to see if they had taken the peanut butter, but the jar was still there. They had opened it though. The lid had been screwed back on crooked…"

Eventually he moved, but the Bigfoot either followed him or another group found him because the visitations haven't stopped. However, after the initial visit he was able to come to terms with the fact that he had big hairy neighbors, but they were friendly and didn't mean him any harm.

"I wake up occasionally in the middle of the night and I can hear what I initially thought were birds singing," he said. "But birds don't sing in the middle of the night."

One night he had friends over, sitting around a fire pit without a fire lit. They all kept hearing a shrill whistle which one of the friends thought was a night bird of some kind. Must be a BIG bird… It doesn't scare him anymore, it just makes him smile.

"I left a melon outside and the next day it was gone and they left me a rock," Gipson said. "It is different from all the other rocks around here."

He said that occasionally he can feel them watching him from the top of the hill, but maybe they don't watch him all of the time because when he got a new propane tank they didn't see it in the middle of the night.

"I think they came to eat some of the apples off of my tree," he said. "Because I could hear them rattling around out there and then heard this 'Oooff' like they just ran into that new tank."

He said he is okay with sharing his fruit with them as long as they leave him a few apples to eat. But the thing that amazes him is that they can split a black walnut in half cleanly.

"I find the shells split open on the seam," he says. "They can even do it while the tough outer hull is still on it, which amazes me!"

He said that he has a grape arbor which is nine feet tall. He normally uses a six foot ladder, standing on the third step, to reach the grapes on top. One day as he was coming home, he glanced over at the grape arbor and noticed that someone was picking the grapes. It didn't bother him, but what hit him later is that what he initially thought was just someone picking the grapes was a Bigfoot – it was picking them with bent arms, standing flat-footed beneath the same arbor he needed a six foot ladder to reach.

He said he has gotten used to seeing them and having them around so much that when they are gone he misses them.

"It's kind of odd, I know, but I miss them when they aren't around as often."

Chris Landon has had two experiences with Bigfoot and they are both interesting. Even now, years later, they stick in his mind and seem slightly unreal.

Rising River

Chris Landon is a pretty big guy, standing at 6 feet four inches and when he was younger, he spent a lot of time outside moving irrigation pipe out in the fields near Morgan Meadows by Rising River. One afternoon during August 1978 he had just finished moving pipe for the day and was driving home alongside the lava flows near the grain field. He had a feeling most of the afternoon he was being watched, but pretty much shook it off. Then on his way home on his four-wheeler he passed a Bigfoot, hunkered down by the sage brush.

He said it was a shock and he wasn't sure he had actually just seen what he thought he saw.

"At first I thought 'WOW! Did I just see what I thought I saw?' I had just glanced over and there he was," Landon said. "I didn't have a place to turn around for about 100 feet and by the time I turned around, he was well across the field."

He said it was really moving fast and seemed to be taking in about eight to ten feet of ground at each stride as it was well into the grain field in the short time it took him to turn around. The other thing that really sticks in his mind was the fact that he could see his hands well above the ripe grain.

"I'm 6'4" and when I move pipe and am standing upright the grain is waist high and my hands are down

75

in the grain," he said. "His hands were at least a foot above the grain."

He said that the Bigfoot was dark black and had brown and yellow eyes. He said he had a feeling of unbelief for several days after the sighting – it really made an impression on him.

Lone Pine

It was deer hunting season in 1997 and Landon was on his way to Lone Pine to go hunting with a friend on a very cold day. They took the road past Mud Lake and were heading across the desert. As they were about 15 or 20 minutes on the east side of Lone Pine they both saw a Bigfoot on the side of the road.
It was after dark in mid-November when they both saw eyes on the side of the road up ahead.

"It was really dark and I thought it might be a cow so we slowed down," Landon said. "We passed it and it was a Bigfoot, crouched down looking like a linebacker, timing his run so he could cross the road."

His partner saw him too, and turned to him and said, "Did you just see that?"

The road was slick so they couldn't maneuver very easily and it took a little bit to turn their rig around and by that time they couldn't see anything. Still, several impressions remain from the experience.

"It had brownish yellow eyes just like the other one, and looked about the same as the other one," he said.

"It was swinging one arm as though to pick up the right timing to cross the road."

He said that he and his hunting partner talked about their experience all the way to their camping spot that night.

"We had both been kind of tired that day, heading out hunting after working a full day of work," he said. "That experience ensured that we were wide awake the rest of the night."

Rose Pond is a reformed gravel pit north of Blackfoot just to the east of Interstate 15. It is a beautiful area and folks who live close by, love being able to play in the water during the summertime. It sits to the side of the Snake River and sports a supply of fish as well as a wooded area nearby that makes it a likely attraction for both kids and Bigfoot. It just happens that the kids ran into the Bigfoot – and more than once. Troy Rider actually ran into the Bigfoot several times back when he didn't know what he was experiencing. Now that he is better educated, he wishes he would happen upon them again.

Rose Pond

Troy Rider is a Blackfoot man who loves the outdoors. When he was younger, he and his friends used to hang out at Rose Pond, mainly just goofing off and wasting time. During one of those little escapades in 1995, a group of them were out with a new shotgun shooting starlings, a small bird that eats a lot of farm grain. He said they were just messing around, throwing rocks, etc, when they were surprised to hear a deep growling and were hit with some sticks. It seemed like a warning, so they moved away from the vicinity. There might have been only one, but it was herding them out of the area. It was dark enough they couldn't see anything in the dark underbrush, but they could definitely hear something.

The next week they were back again at night with a group of seven - guys and girls - just goofing off. The guys wanted to frighten the girls, so they walked them around the archery range where they had experienced the deep growling noise the week before.

"We were walking along the river when we saw what looked like a big beaver laying in the middle of the road," Rider said, "It was bent over real weird, possibly on its knees, touching its toes." He pointed it out to one of his friends, "Look at that beaver!"

Rider said that they were out in the moonlight about 11 pm, in late August, and could see fairly clearly. It was about 30 to 40 feet away from them and as Rider spoke, he started hearing a funny bird whistling sound, sounding like it surrounded them. The supposed beaver, actually a juvenile Bigfoot, startled and stood up acting like it was in trouble.

"I remember that it was fast, and had a wide chest. It leaned forward as it ran." Rider said. "It looked like it was running on its tiptoes. It was kind of jerky, and very fast."

He said that the Bigfoot took three steps up the embankment and disappeared into the river – it didn't slow down at all.
One of the girls in the group ran back up the river bank hysterically. The guys didn't want to admit it, but they were scared too.

Pass Creek

Rider and a friend were elk hunting above Mackay at a camp called Loristica near Pass Creek in October 2002 and had been there for six days without seeing anyone else. In the middle of the night, about 4 or 4:30 the second night, they awoke to a distinct smell, a very bad smell, "Like something musky or dead – only three times worse," Rider said. "When we would move, the smell would leave."

Stuff went missing off their table at night – about 20 geodes, silverware, and a pocket knife. His friend kept blaming him for the stuff disappearing, but Rider knew he hadn't taken it.
There were two bucks hanging up in the tree, but they weren't disturbed.

A group of guys, on horseback, carrying CB radios, rode past Rider and his friend. He heard them say they saw something that looked like a bear but they weren't going to shoot it. They weren't sure what it was, but they were telling each other to be careful. That was after two nights of the smell so Rider and his friend were already on the alert.

Sawmill Canyon

Rider was camping at a family reunion in June of 2002. He woke up in the middle of the night and could smell something horrible. His first concern was for the kids that were camping in a smaller tent outside his bigger tent. He figured his dogs would have barked a warning or something, but the dogs weren't even disturbed. He couldn't find his flashlight so he got the camp stove (a wood burning unit inside the tent), going. As soon as the logs started burning, the Bigfoot and the smell were gone.

"It's real pretty up there," Rider said. "There is a lot of water and trees; it is really beautiful. You come out of that canyon and it opens up into the desert so I imagine it was nice for them up there."

Blackfoot Reservoir

A few years later in October 2003 Rider was near Blackfoot Reservoir with a friend hunting elk. He was there about two days before his friend came up and then stayed another couple of days when he had another encounter with the Bigfoot only this time he didn't get a clear look at it. It just happened that it grabbed hold of the corner pole of their tent and shook it.

"We didn't see anything, but it sure startled us," he said.

This time, unlike last time, he had his flashlight with him and he turned it on. He clearly saw a hand come down and grab the corner of the tent and shake their 12 x 12 square tent.
Meanwhile, in a whispering voice, his friend said he could hear something outside the tent. This time he didn't smell anything and didn't see anything. They looked the next morning for some kind of a sign of Bigfoot, but the ground was frozen and what grass there was, was matted down where the men had been walking the day before. That was the last time anything happened and it still puzzles Rider.

"I still wonder why I have seen them so often and haven't seen them since. It kind of puzzles me."

What does he think about Bigfoot? Is he just lucky, blessed or cursed to keep having these experiences with the Bigfoot?

"There for a while, I thought I was cursed to keep running into them," he said. We didn't have the Internet back then so I really didn't know what Bigfoot was, only what I learned on TV. When the horrible smell came, I didn't know what to expect so my first instinct was a fear-based adrenaline rush." Now Rider would like to see the Bigfoot again but hasn't for a while.

"I kind of wonder how many people have these experiences, but don't ever say anything to someone – they just keep it silent and don't talk about it."

It is surprising to find two siblings who have both had experiences with the big guy, but such is the case here. Wendy Lamb is Troy Rider's sister and has had her own experience with Bigfoot. She makes the comment that she saw her brother Troy after his experience with the Bigfoot and he was really shook up. Her own experience happened on a family camping excursion out past Howe.

Sawmill Canyon

It was late August in 2005 and the Lamb family was having their annual camping trip up Sawmill Canyon which is about 40 minutes past Howe. It was later in the evening and the family was cooking their supper over a fire. The kids were running around and playing and everything seemed fine until the hot dogs started disappearing faster than they should have.

"My son was five and my nephew was two and they were playing and we were cooking," Lamb said. "I noticed that all of the hot dogs had disappeared so I asked my son if he knew what had happened to all of them."

He said, "We gave them to our friend."

She said she questioned him pretty good.

"Where is your friend?"
"In the back of the truck," he said.

She said that about then it really shook her as there had been some bears sighted not too long before their trip near the area they were camped. Several of the adults in the party went to check the back of the pickup the boy pointed to but all they found was an area where the dust had been wiped clean in the back.

"We looked around with flashlights, but didn't see anything, but that area has a lot of trees and it felt a little weird out there, like someone was watching us," she said. "Later that night we knew something climbed into that truck because the hitch would screech. We checked it each time, but didn't see anything."

She said they went back near the fire and questioned her son some more, asking him what he had been doing with the hot dogs and whether he was scared.

"He said it had hands – he didn't put the hot dog in its mouth, he gave it to its hand," she said. "He said they were pretending that they were running a restaurant, feeding their customers, and it didn't scare them at all – they were having fun with a friend."

Later that night when everyone went to bed there was a disturbance and they knew that the Bigfoot hadn't really left the area.

"Something was knocking on the tent, hitting it," Lamb said. "You could hear it shuffling around outside. We didn't ever see anything after that, but I was jittery and scared that whole trip. My son wasn't the least bit scared though."

Even years later when the family brought up the subject of the Bigfoot on this particular trip, this young man assures them that it had hands just like his and it wasn't scary at all.

86

Admittedly, there have been a lot of sightings of the big guy on the Fort Hall Reservation. That might be because there are more of them there, but it might also be because people pay attention to the area around them more. Either way, Susan Denny has had a few encounters with different Bigfoot when they come past her farm.

Snake River Bottoms

The area where Susan Denny lives is fairly remote and beautiful. Not many people travel out that way, but from time to time she has visitors who leave a big impression.

"I was home by myself one day and could hear and smell something outside the house, bumping against it," she said. "My dog came in the house and was just freaking out."

She said she was careful to move away from the windows as she was afraid something would reach in and grab her, but in time it moved away.
She has an older apple tree in the orchard behind her home and one particular year she hadn't been able to get out to them until a lot of them had fallen off the tree onto the ground. The tree itself has more weeds than grass around it and she said when she finally made it out to take care of the apples she found all of the weeds around the tree had been smashed down and walked upon.

"All of the fallen apples were gone," she said. "You could see where the weeds had been smashed down about ten feet out from the tree and there was a big pile of poop that looked like human poop only bigger."

She said she also found some really long smelly hair hanging on the barbed wire fence by the tree and initially thought about having someone run a DNA analysis on it but after some thought decided not to.

"I didn't want anyone hunting it," she said. "So one day I just let the wind carry it away."

She said that she has several fruit trees in the orchard behind her home besides the apples including apricots, peaches, and crab apples and each year she leaves fruit on the trees for the Bigfoot.

"We never pick them bald," She said. "When you think about it, they have to struggle to survive too; I can at least help them out some."

Another experience happened near the fourth of July one year when she had her grandkids over at her house lighting off fireworks. She said she could sense that something was outside the yard just watching them and possibly enjoying the fireworks like everyone else. That changed once they let off the Piccolo Pete's.

"All of a sudden we heard a big ruckus coming across the field, knocking the irrigation pipes around," she said. "Those Piccolo Pete's are really shrill and I think it got agitated by the shrill noise."

The next day when her husband went out with her to the field, they found the stack of irrigation pipes knocked all helter-skelter – not neatly stacked like they had been left.

In 2013 she had an experience about two o'clock in the morning when she could hear a Bigfoot coming down the wheel line (irrigation pipe) in the field behind her home and across the road. It had something it was hitting or tapping the line with all the way down the field.

"My husband wanted to drive over there but I said no way," she said.

She said they were out checking the irrigation water one night and saw a big man figure wading through the water from a distance.

"There was no reason for a man to be out there," she said.

Tilden Bridge is on the north end of the Fort Hall Indian Reservation and the area where it crosses the Snake River is known to be a good fishing and hunting spot. Bruce Wiggins was hunting ducks on this particular trip, but it wasn't very productive. Unfortunately, he must have disturbed the resident Bigfoot because he wanted him GONE.

Tilden Bridge

"I was on the north side of Tilden Bridge between Thomas and Tilden, duck hunting in a duck blind," Wiggins said. "I was just sitting there when all of a sudden the water in the river about twenty feet ahead of me just shot up out of the river about the height of a house!"

He said it scared him; the sound was so sudden and intense.

"Initially I thought that some kid must be throwing rocks to make it splash," he said. "I looked across the river and it was too far to throw a rock."

His car was a mile and a half down the river, but he figured that whatever was out there, it didn't want him there so he started back towards the car. All along the way back, he felt that someone was watching him.

"It scared me enough I put another shell in my gun," he said.

At one point he had to cross a tributary and pass a pond that was pretty big. He carefully went past the willows and went up a small hill, grateful that he was out of the bottoms. And then it happened again.

"I saw a big black something, flying through the air and then splash in the middle of the pond," he said. "When I first saw it, I thought it was a diving bird, but both times they were BIG rocks."

He said he hasn't ever seen what was throwing the rocks, but there was no question in his mind, but that it was something big, nothing else could have thrown that big of rock with that much force, that far.

"I figure it wanted me to leave its territory," he said. "You can't blame them for wanting peace."

When you grow up in Idaho you can't help but hear about Bigfoot growing up. Damon Irons is no different. He said that when he was a kid, he was fascinated by the many stories he heard. He figured they must be real; there were too many stories for it to be otherwise. But he truly became a Bigfoot Believer the day he saw one himself.

Wallowa Mountains

It was a beautiful day in July 2010 when Damon Irons set out to travel from Boise to Joseph, Oregon on his motorcycle.

"I wasn't in any hurry so I took all of the back roads," Irons said. "I don't know if you have ever ridden a motorcycle, but you spend a lot of time looking at and evaluating the road ahead, especially since the road was a paved forest service road."

He said it was the middle of the week and he had the whole place to himself and he was surprised at how plentiful the vegetation was – it looked kind of like rain forest. As he gained in elevation he noticed that it was getting drier with more pine trees. He was traveling on one flat stretch of road about seven PM with terrain rising on the left of the road and falling away on the right side. There were straight lodge pole pines lined up almost symmetrically and he was checking the road when he noticed something dark move in the trees ahead of him.

"It appeared for a moment, then disappeared, then reappeared," he said.

93

He slowed down and right where there was a ten foot gap in the trees, he saw his first Bigfoot.

"He had his back to me and was standing in the barrow pit, but even sitting on the road above him on my motorcycle he was taller than I was," Irons said. "He was really dark grey with broad shoulders with his arms hanging straight down."

He said that the length of his arms surprised him, that and the shape of his head which wasn't what he expected.

"I stopped my bike about fifteen feet ahead of where I had seen him and yelled, 'Very clever, I wouldn't have seen you if you hadn't moved!' and then kept talking," he said. "I walked back to where I had seen it, but nothing was there and the adrenalin was wearing off."

He stood there and looked around and then heard big heavy footprints going up the hill behind him but didn't see the Bigfoot again.
A while later camping in McCall he thought he heard one in the middle of the night.

"I heard a long drawn out 'Whoop' out across the trees," he said. "I couldn't see anything so it might have been one, but then it might also have been some kids out there just squatchin around."

Rod Teel is one of those guys who has seen and done a lot with his life. He is a retired army man who currently battles fires all over as a fireman with Teton County Fire. This particular experience happened while in the area above Bone called Wayan off of Tin Cup road.

Wayan

Rod Teel and his friends and family have been going out elk hunting to the same location for the last thirty years. Last year he invited some of his former army buddies out for a hunting adventure in the same spot.

"They come from all over the United States," he said. "We really look forward to this time of the year."

He said it was about ten or ten thirty at night and they had pulled their ATV's into a circle and were just sitting there talking and shooting the breeze. Suddenly they heard a cream that resembled nothing else they had ever heard. The ten adults in the group all looked at each other and said, "What the HECK was that?"

"I have never heard anything like that before or since for that matter," Teel said. "I've been in the woods a LOT – both as a hunter and a fireman and I have never heard anything like that before."

He said that when he is working a fire, animals will often come past the firemen in the smoke and he often hears all sorts of animal sounds through the noise of the particular fire they are working. As a hunter, he has also heard a lot of animals – cats, wolves, elk, etc – but nothing quite like what they heard that night.

"We heard it several times, each time getting closer to us," he said. "It was enough to convince me that there was a Bigfoot out there – it scared the heck out of me!"

He said for the first time ever, everyone decided they would rather sleep somewhere else that night – no one stayed out on the mountain. The funny thing is that they are now planning this year's excursion and he still doesn't have any takers to sleep out under the stars.

"I was talking to one of my buddies just the other day and he was telling me how excited he was to come hunting," Teel said. "I asked him if he was going to sleep outside and he said 'heck no!' Somehow I can't blame him!"

CONCLUSION

After reading this book you might believe in Bigfoot, but then again, you might not. There is plenty of evidence to suggest that there is something out there that needs further investigation. I am positive that there are many other stories of encounters that have happened here in our great state but maybe they haven't been told yet.

I welcome the opportunity to hear your story and maybe it will be included in the next book…

Please contact me: becky@beckycookonline.com

APPENDIX

There are multiple website with additional information on Bigfoot. I am listing a few of these here.
www.bigfootencounters.com
www.bigfootlunchclub.com
www.bfro.net
www.texasbigfoot.com
www.gcbro.com
www.oregonbigfoot.com
www.bigfootsightings.org

Almost every state has some type of a Bigfoot sightings organization, yet Idaho does not. Some of the sightings from Idaho are reported on other websites, most notably those on www.bfro.net (Bigfoot Research Organization)

This footprint was found in the Stinky Creek area up near Palisades Dam in 2013

This footprint is one of the ones found by Dale Graham in Basin Patch.

ABOUT THE AUTHOR

Becky Cook is an Idaho native who loves to write. She has written for numerous newspapers and magazines throughout the western United States and has reported local, regional, and national news. She has been fascinated with Bigfoot sightings and stories all her life and it is the favorite subject for her eight children as well. The Bigfoot stories have delighted many of her friends and family for many years, and now they are being retold here for you – her readers.

This book is the first of several books telling the stories of the Bigfoot. If you have had a sighting and would like to share that information, please contact her: becky@beckycookonline.com

ABOUT THE ARTIST

Brandon Tennant was born in Miles City, Montana and raised in West Yellowstone, Idaho. He has been drawing all of his life. He became interested in Bigfoot when he was a kid and first heard of a sighting in his area. He drew the picture used on the cover, originally titled, "Patty Lives" based on the Bigfoot seen by the Patterson group on October 27, 1967 and with verification from other folks who have seen Bigfoot in person. What you are seeing is a very close likeness to the Bigfoot found in Idaho.
He and his wife and sons live in Pocatello, Idaho where he runs Falling Rock Productions and Sasquatchprints.com.